How I  young at 42

How

I'm

Beating depression

http://www.fast-print.net/bookshop

HOW I LOOK SO YOUNG AT 42
HOW I'M BEATING DEPRESSION
Copyright © Dawn Cousins 2015

A catalogue record for this book is available from the British Library

ISBN 978-178456-276-2

First published 2015 by
FASTPRINT PUBLISHING
Peterborough, England.

I'm too blessed
To be getting
stressed

Invest a little more
in yourself
And a little less in
others

About me

I was abandoned at birth which led to the first seven years of my life in and out of a variety of children's homes, nurseries and foster homes. I was eventually adopted at the age of seven, which was not a positive experience and I left home at fifteen. I did a whole circle and I was taken back into the care system after several run ins with the police at fifteen.

I'm now the grand old age of 42 and a single woman with four beautiful children. Well, I say children, they are now all over 16. Although raising four children has been a rocky road at times I don't regret one second of it. I'm very proud of how they have all turned out and I love them dearly. Being a devoted mother to my children has been a major part of my life for over 22 years and will continue to be so. Although I'm a single Mother and suffering from depression, I find working part time helps me to feel like I'm contributing towards society like everyone else.

I have been taking prescribed medication for depression, for some time now. I've kept my illness undercover from those closest and dearest to me. Mainly to protect them from feeling uncomfortable and lost for words, as well as to hide my shame and embarrassment. I'm still taking gradual positive steps forward at my own pace, day by day to begin to reduce my medication and embrace a happier and more positive me. I decided to share my personal experiences and helpful suggestions with you, to help both myself and hopefully others. My life has not been text book so far and I now have learnt to accept and embrace who Dawn Cousins is and what I have to offer the world. Although I have had a troubled childhood, rocky relationships, never lived with a partner or walked down the isle or owned my own property, with my hand on my heart I can say I have been truly blessed. I was searching for a book that gives simple practical advice that someone like myself could relate to. I didn't want to be bombarded with technical jargon, I just wanted some clear, practical and simple strategies that I could possibly try out. I have been a silent sufferer for so long it has become an invisible mask that was blocking my road to a positive recovery and brighter future. Not being in a good place both emotionally and mentally for so long has been a major barrier on the direction of my life so far. I am proud to say I am dyslexic and unique in many ways that give me my individuality. I found certain methods of engaging and progressing are not suitable for everyone, as we are all different. So although I have tried a variety of professional methods to overcome my depression, I realised my true road to a brighter future was waiting patiently within myself.

There isn't a day that goes by when I'm not asked my age. Everyone's reaction is always either, "I don't believe you "or "How do you look so young?". These are the most common responses I receive from both males and females, young and old. People of all ages always ask me my secret to raising four children and remaining so youthful at heart and astoundingly young looking. Through personal experiences I have been able to achieve a youthful body, mind and soul as well as being able to look nearly half my age. So here is an insight into how I have been able to put the aging process on pause naturally and remain young, happy and wrinkle free. I'm not medically trained or a health or beauty professional so please remember to seek professional advice when necessary.

Don't be afraid or ashamed to seek help and guidance in your time of need!

The unseen & unspoken illness

The dreaded D and M words (depression & mental health) still remain a big taboo even in this modern day and age, even with celebrities, sports personalities and other well-known faces opening up about their own personal battles with mental health. I strongly believe that if everyone from children to adults, male to females, felt comfortable and open enough to discuss mental health issues, this would benefit so many unnecessarily silent sufferers.

Depression affects so many people from a wide range of cultures and backgrounds with an enormous stigma still attached to mental health. It has become an illness to feel ashamed to be associated with. Depression isn't a comfortable topic at any social gathering or work place I've attended. The awkwardness and doom quickly fills the room and the sudden dash to get a drink or a trip to the loo, is a quick escape for those who are most uncomfortable with the topic of conversation.

I personally would never dare tick the box on an application form when asked 'do you have any mental health conditions?' Just the thought of people I could be potentially working with knowing I have a mental health illness sends my heart pumping through my chest. I also believe that if I were to tick that box, the chances of getting the job would drastically drop. Since I have never ticked that box I can't comment on the reaction or questions that would follow a thorough read of my application form.

When I came up with the title of my book, my heart was pacing for both the positive and negative reasons.

Negative reasons-

1 - OMG! What will people that know me think about me, now they know my dirty little secret?

2 - My long covered up and embarrassing secret will be out there for all to see, where can I hide?

3 - Will my kids be ashamed of their mum and get negative feedback from their peers?

4 - People will judge the book by its cover and not feel comfortable reading it.

As fast as the negative thoughts and utter dread entered my mind the positive and feisty side quickly found its voice.

Positive reasons-

1 - You have nothing to be ashamed of!

2 - Think of all those other silent sufferers you'll be speaking out for!

3 - Your courage and words could help others just like you!

4 - Help remove the stigma of mental health and be proud of yourself.

5 - Everyone has personal experiences that others could benefit from.

6 - You have a wealth of life experience that so many others can benefit from and relate to.

So here are my simple coping strategies and ideas that I hope you will find helpful. Dealing with depression is a slow and gradual process that takes a lot of courage, inner strength and perseverance. There are many forms of depression and no two people are the same.

Life is an ongoing journey with many paths,

Sometimes a u turn is necessary to make a fresh start

My children saved my life

A fter years of being told to stop feeling sorry for myself and just get on with things, hiding my suffering behind a big smile and putting on a brave face quickly became second nature. From a young age the feeling of sadness, loneliness and having negative thoughts was what I knew. It was what I thought it was a normal way of life for me. So as the same dark cloud remained firmly over my head as I went into adulthood, I kept my suffering to myself. I remember there was one occasion that I couldn't hold the tears and the cry for help hidden any longer. A family member was due to drop her daughter at my house for me to babysit for her, so I had no choice but to open the door and try and mask my pain. My eyes were so puffy and my whole body language spoke for itself. She had turned up with her partner and as always was the life and soul. I had tried to explain to her that I wasn't feeling well and I wasn't up for babysitting. She wasn't having any of it and begged me to stick to the prearranged plan. As I tried to express how I was feeling, my emotions got the better of me and I couldn't hold back the tears from streaming down my face any longer. With her partner being a witness to all of this, I was quickly ushered upstairs out of sight. I was handed a screwed up bunch of loo paper and told to stop crying and making a show of myself in front of her partner. The guy shouted from the bottom of the stairs if I was alright. It was with the answer to that question, I knew I had to continue to suffer in silence. "She's fine, just had some bad news', she positively shouted back at him. On days when I would find it a struggle to hide my sadness I would just cut myself off from the outside world and deal with it alone. I would lie and say I was busy, working or even physically ill just to avoid contact with the outside world. I just didn't have the will power to make others believe I was alright. Some days I just buried my head in a pillow, drew the curtains and isolated myself from the outside world. There was actually a time when I couldn't see a brighter future and actually planned to take my own life. There was no fear in ending my life, I felt so worthless I just wanted to remove myself from the world. The fact that I had nobody to turn to in my darkest hour and I didn't know I was suffering from an actual illness, made my decision to end my life even more urgent. Seeking help from my doctor never even crossed my mind, why would it? I wasn't suffering from an actual physical illness. As I sat in my car in an isolated car park I felt it was definitely my time to go. I just wanted to block out all the sadness and negative feelings that were troubling me for so very long. I just wanted to sleep, just fall into a deep peaceful sleep without having to wake up and face my daily challenge of just living. I calmly bought some pain killers and sat in the car with tears flowing down my face. I could only see one way out and this was it. I was always a person that thought of others before myself and made sure everyone else's needs were met. I then had the realisation that I had four innocent children to provide for, who would look after them and love them in a way only I could? I couldn't do that to them and for the love of my children, I started driving home with the same dark cloud over my head.

I wasn't sure what help the doctor could offer me, would she just laugh and say stop wasting her time? I didn't even know how to start to describe how I was feeling or what was wrong with me. I didn't want to book an appointment when there could be someone with a real illness who needs to be seen. I had to try as I knew I couldn't go on living like this any longer. As I started to put into words the negative thoughts, nonstop crying and the continuous feeling of feeling lethargic, the tears poured down my face. The doctor was a mature woman with a passive but direct approach. She knew I was raising four children and they were all young at the time. As she gently passed the tissue box in my direction, she informed me I was suffering from depression and with the combination of medication and counselling I would be fine over time. As she shiftily swivelled her large black office chair around, she started tapping away at the keyboard. I was taken aback that there was actually a prescription that could help with my nonstop feeling of sadness and thoughts of suicide. The doctor made it very clear that I must attend counselling alongside taking the medication as the two go hand in hand.

We all deserve
happiness
But we all don't
realise we deserve
it

If you can think it!

And you truly believe it!

You certainly can achieve it!

The strongest of us
are usually the most
sensitive

Return to sender

I'm naturally a happy person with a huge bubbly personality and a wide smile on my face. I'm not suggesting that everyone suffering from depression walks around with their head hung low and uncontrollable tears streaming down their face. I come across as having a very strong and courageous persona but that is not always a true reflection of how I'm feeling inside. When I'm feeling low this can have a detrimental effect on me. My mood can drop from having an average day to having a nightmare day.

I come across as a strong character from the outside but inside I am a sensitive soul. In the past I have taken other people's criticism and interpretation of myself to heart. Not only have I taken every word as a negative interpretation, I have rerun their words over and over again. I've then stored them and added them to an already lengthy catalogue of self-disbelief in a vault in my mind.

I've learnt over the years there are always going to be people that have a variety of opinions of me and will not be shy in coming forward and airing their views. What is important for my mental health and my overall well being, is how I deal with it and if I allow their words to win and bring me down. I call it return to sender with a first class stamp on it and a signature required. I'll literally write a personal positive letter to that person and then cut it up in small pieces and recycle it. That is my way of getting all their negativity out of my head and saying that is your opinion of me and your words will not be bringing me down. I don't and will not give you my time, energy or even care to digest your opinions of me. There is no approval needed to how I live my life, I refuse to focus on others when my time is precious to me. I will no longer allow other people's negativity to play a part in moving my life forward on the path to a positive and fulfilling life.

Those who fear
fulfilling their own
dreams

Fear those who do

Don't allow others
to be the director
in your life!

Who is the boss of you?

Your brain!

- Yes your brain works relentlessly to keep you in tip top form. The brain has so many functions from controlling our thinking to our patterns of behaviour. Looking after our brains is just as important as maintaining a variety of activities for our bodies.
- Regular mental activities that challenge your brain by developing new and interesting skills, are a great way to giving your brain a workout. Stimulating your brain in a variety of positive ways keeps it remaining sharp and powered up. Learning a new language, even if it is one to a few words a day is a great way to keep your brain working for you.
- It's very important to maintain a good social life, which incorporates having fun and feeling happy. Interacting with others is what we as humans require and mixing with positive people is a great way to lift our mood.
- There are many negative triggers and lifestyle choices that can lead to feeling low and restrict us from fulfilling our true potential in life.

- Avoid smoking, including passive smoking!
- Avoid taking all forms of drugs!
- Avoid drinking too much alcohol!
- Keep stress levels to a minimum!
- Include a variety of brain foods in your daily diet!
- Avoid watching too much television each day!
- Avoid being swallowed up by social media!
- Avoid indulging in too much junk food and processed foods!
- Avoid surrounding yourself with negative people and environments!

The world has so many choices available to us

Making the right
choices can take a
lifetime to master

How was your day?

Negative day-

I had a really rubbish day today. It poured with rain, I felt miserable from the time I woke up till I finally got to bed. The kids were stressing me out, as usual.

Positive day-

I had a good day today. Got a chance to wear my funky (I don't care) wellies. They reminded me of happy rainy days as a child. The kids were being kids, so I took my five minutes timeout to breathe and recharged my batteries. Played hide and seek followed by sleeping lions that worked a treat. Watched a comedian on my phone before bed, she was so funny. All in all a good fun day all round.

Top 10 tips to becoming happy

1 - Try and leave your home daily, even for a brisk walk around the block.

2 - Avoid sticking to the same daily routine. If you always travel to a certain destination via the same route, switch it up when possible.

3 - Start a conversation or exchange a simple hello or goodbye with a stranger or someone that has a bubbly and positive persona about them.

4 - Watch or listen to something that makes you smile or laugh, even if it's only for a few minutes a day.

5 - Keep track of your happiness, while avoiding people and situations that have a negative effect on you.

6 - Start believing in yourself and the achievements you can accomplish in your life.

7 - Change "I can't", to *"I can, or I can damn well give it my all"*

8 - Take each day as a brand new start and don't be hard on yourself when things don't go to plan.

9 - Continue to invest in new discoveries and self development.

10 - Start to own your life and your place in the world.

Life is a balancing act,

Discover the right balance that works for you.

123 Plan

I was always a yes, yes, yes person since I can remember, I believe this stems from my childhood pattern of always wanting to please those around me in return for their love and acceptance. The word yes used to be on autopilot, I didn't even need to hear the end of the person's question or requirements and I had spluttered out the word. Everyone knew I would say YES!, even putting others and their problems before myself and my children. I would do my utmost to help those in their hour of need, so nobody expected that Dawn the good listener, the agony aunt, the joker, the confidante would have her own demons, battles, highs and lows and be suffering from a mental health illness. I portrayed a very strong exterior and asking for support and a friend in my hour of need was a struggle for me.

I became bogged down with other people's requirements and issues which was taking a toll on not only my emotional wellbeing but my mental and physical health too. It was as if I was trying to balance my own life, while allowing everyone else to pile on their crap. The scales always seemed to be tipping in their favour and my life was put on a back burner or last to do on the to do list. I ended up burnt out and in a very dark place where I couldn't see the light or an exit sign with a bright future with my name on it, anywhere in sight.

I came up with the 123 plan when I was beginning to say yes to people even though I knew I would literally have to spilt myself in two to fulfil their needs. As I started applying my 123 rule I felt like I was finally starting to take some control of my time and my life. I was prioritising Dawn for once, not everyone else. I knew I couldn't suddenly turn into a selfish and non-caring person as that isn't who I am. At the same time I knew saying yes to everyone was making me feel low and adding an extra strain on my shoulders.

1 - I would calmly listen to what the person was asking of me.

2 - I would tell them I would get back to them when I've had time to think about it.

3 - I would think about it in my own time with no time pressure to respond. When I had thought about it I would let them know my final decision.

This has worked wonders for reducing the stress and unburdening me with the worries or needs of others. I'm no longer wearing myself thin, trying to be everyone's saviour. At first people were taken aback by my new reaction and the fact that I wasn't always at the end of the phone for their every whim. Then they were asking if everything was okay with me or if had they upset me in some way. They asked why I hadn't been to see them or been in touch for so long. Nothing was wrong, finally everything was right! I was putting myself first and not rushing around like a headless chicken after everyone else. I felt free, relaxed and as if a heavy load had been craned off my shoulders. As a reminder and to avoid slipping back into my yes sir no sir mode, I have a 123 image on my phone's screen saver, so there is a constant reminder.

Don't allow the pressure & negative vibes of others to affect how you live your life.

Yesterday, today and tomorrow

My mind used to race around like a hare on adrenalin at times, while my body would struggle to keep up. I believed I had to fit a hundred and one things in one day just to feel like I had accomplished something at the end of the day. There wouldn't be a day that went by without something or someone needing my attention. I would find myself stressing over things that happened in my past and allowing them to play mind games in my future. For example, being a single mother, I would pray that this didn't happen to my children and yet their child bearing days are a long way away. Yet I'm thinking about having to support them and how I can shield them from the emotional pain that I suffered. On top of that there would be the minor daily issues that I would allow to get me down or see them in a negative light. The long list of tomorrow's concerns would start running havoc through my head. I ended up not being able to just live day to day and enjoy just being in the present moment and remaining positive about the future. I would feel so totally drained and deflated that I had no energy for myself or my children. So now I don't worry or focus on the past as yesterday has come and gone. I wake up each day with a positive outlook about the day ahead and I remain focused and enjoy the present day. I keep an up to date diary so each day I can see what appointments I have and this also helps to remove a lot of unnecessary stress. I also make a reasonable to do list each day, so my head is not over cluttered with things to do.

Everyone has issues.
The key is <u>*not*</u>
To allow their
issues to become
your issues!

Time to check in

Monitoring ourselves is essential to remaining positive, happy and continuing to live our lives the way we choose. Living fast paced lives with so many obstacles and everyday day things to fit in, we can easily neglect ourselves. At times we are probably not even aware of this. It's similar to gaining weight, those extra pounds didn't just happen overnight, it was a slow and gradual weight gain, the odd drink here and there or the sneaky biscuit now and then. Before long our clothes begin to feel a little snug around the waistline.

By taking timeout to check in with ourselves is a great way to make sure we are still moving forward in a positive direction. It's similar to going to the doctor or dentist for a routine check up.

Here are a few simple questions to ask yourself now and then.

- Am I keeping up with my physical activities?
- How am I feeling, emotionally, psychically and mentally?
- Am I making positive steps forward, to achieving my chosen goals and becoming a happier person?
- Am I powering up my brain by engaging in a variety of self development and mental stimulation activities?
- Am I feeding myself a well balanced variety of foods?
- When did I last socialise with new and interesting people?
- What direction is my life going at this present time?

- Am I getting adequate sleep?
- When did I last treat myself?
- Have I been laughing and smiling regularly?

My daily check in notes

My weekly check in notes

My monthly check in notes.

My yearly check in notes.

We all have
baggage.
It all depends
how we carry it

Keep life simple!

Keep motivated!

Keep focused!

Keep things
moving forward!

Keep true to
yourself!

Keep positive!

Dawn Cousins

Putting realistic action into achieving goals

K now what you want as an individual and start to put positive steps in place to become a happier and goal achieving person. It is all well and good in saying I want to achieve all these goals and I have dreams and desires to be like this or that. You can write lists after lists and visualise all you like, don't get me wrong, there is nothing wrong with that. Unless you put effort, determination and consistency into achieving your dreams, they are more likely to remain just that, dreams.

Here is an example of how I personally intend to achieve my goal of finding love. It might not be a wow factor for most but due to my own personal journey, finding love is a major mountain for me to climb.

Finding Love

✓ Make a clear and simple decision to find love.
✓ I need to feel happy and content in my own skin.
✓ Discover and get to know who I am as a unique individual before I start to learn about another person.
✓ Know what I have to offer in a relationship.
✓ Decide what I am looking for within a relationship.
✓ Be honest and realistic in choosing a future partner that complements me.
✓ Know my likes and my dislikes in a future partner, learn from past relationships.
✓ Be able to make a confident decision in love.
✓ Avoid the urgency to be loved and needed to lead to making the wrong choices in love.
✓ Decide my own boundaries within a relationship.
✓ Don't feel under pressure to satisfy the needs and requirements of the other person.
✓ Don't base failed past relationships on future ones.
✓ Maintain an open and positive mind.
✓ Don't give up!

I am not so Isolated

I solation can lead to a whole lot of time to overthink all kinds of negative thoughts and images. It can encourage bad habits to raise their ugly heads as well as low moods. I made the decision to withdraw from both my biological family as well as my adoptive family. This was a hard decision to make and didn't happen overnight. I knew I was engaging in unhealthy relationships with family members that were making my depression worse at times and holding me back from living a happier and positive lifestyle. Removing myself from what I had been forcing myself to believe was a supportive and loving environment that I needed in my life, has been a struggle but a decision I don't regret at all. We all need to feel like we have the love of others and company around us and of course, family should be the main source of unconditional love we require. The unconditional love of my family came at a price that I had been paying for too long, reflecting back it was probably so I didn't feel isolated. I felt like I had finally broken free and a massive weight had been lifted off my shoulders. I was finally able to start to discover who I truly was and put myself first for a change.

As I started to reflect on my life I realised there were often times I felt lonely and isolated. My children were becoming young adults and more independent and I was having more time to myself.

I'm a person that thrives on engaging with others and I'm at my happiest when mixing with all walks of life. Nothing and no amount of money can buy having a good old laugh and enjoying good company.

I'm lucky I'm confident enough to be able to join a new social activity, so that is exactly what I did. I started looking into hobbies and interests and I just went along. I'm not saying it was easy, there were times I just wanted to stay at home and go into zombie mode in front of the telly. I knew it would benefit me both mentally as well as physically to make the effort.

The good side of that was I was able to go in and out, if I chose to engage and build friendship I had the choice to do so. There was no pressure to get caught up in big discussions and swap numbers.

The key for me was to break the isolation pattern that I was finding myself falling quickly into. By just being in the company of others made a real positive change for me. I started to really feel the positive benefits of not isolating myself from the outside world.

Don't wait for others to praise you,

It could be a long wait

Work to live

not

live to work

Stuck in the mud

I was finding myself stuck in the same place or repeating habits that were playing a negative role in my life. I would seek for change and a brighter day, yet my actions would always lead me back to an unhappy place. I felt like I was often finding myself stuck in the mud and the only person that was able to pull me out was me. The very same person that got stuck in the mud in the first place. I started to look at the people I had contact with and how our relationships were affecting me. Was it a positive one? One I truly needed in my life? Or was it having a negative effect on my wellbeing? So as I was paying more attention to the company I was keeping I decided that some of the company I kept was no longer a positive energy. I was holding onto friendships and relationships for the wrong reasons. Times had moved forward but I was stuck in my ways from previous years and these patterns were not healthy ones.

With so many methods of communicating these days, it was easy enough for me to distance myself and take control over the kind of unhealthy relationships I was having. This was a new experience for me and I was finding it very therapeutic. People come and people go during our lives and once I discovered I wasn't the same person as months or even years ago, I had to move on. I also had to really start to consider the unhealthy environments I would consistently find myself in. To avoid getting stuck in the mud again and again, I had to take time to discover the changes required in my life.

During our lives
people
Come and go as we
all need to
continue to grow

Mirror Mirror on the wall

I know this might sound a little crazy but try it continuously for 30 days. After that you should get into a pattern of really loving and appreciating the person in the mirror; YOU! I tell my children I love them after phone calls, in text messages and when we say goodbye on a daily basis. This might seem a little over the top but you will be surprised how much this can have a positive effect. Growing up, those three little words would have made such a difference to me in so many ways. I would have felt loved, contented, and able to look in the mirror and feel proud to be me.

How many of us really take the time to look in the mirror and say 'I really love being who I am, I love who I am as a person, the way I look" and an array of other positive compliments. We could and should all be paying ourselves positive compliments on a daily basis.

We are all very quick and experts at criticising ourselves when we look in the mirror. I don't like this and that about my body, we hardly appreciate who that wonderful person is looking back at us.

A generous &
creative heart

=

a loving & caring
heart

Record it to avoid it!

I find keeping a progress diary really helps me to avoid repeating unhealthy choices that I could easily repeat time and time again. Keeping a progress diary for me is helpful in keeping myself moving forward and making positive changes that work for me and my mental health. I found it good practice to keep a record so I can see positive changes within myself and to be able to do continuous self-development checks. Here's an example before I started keeping a progress diary.

Relationship-

I met a guy online and we started dating, things started moving rapidly and I was just focused on the end result. I was so determined this guy was the one and my fairy tale happy ending was finally here. I was oblivious to the tell tale signs and the negative patterns I was falling into. Firstly the unhealthy signs from the guy I was blinded to see and secondly I was allowing myself to fall into the same unhealthy patterns. I was starting to feel overwhelmed, restricted, confused, emotionally drained and worst of all, I was putting his needs before mine. If I had been monitoring myself and had a record that I could refer to, things wouldn't have gotten so on top of me.

My record it to avoid it notes

We all learn and develop in different ways, Find out the ways that work for you

Feed yourself right
to
feel right!

The best things in life are truly free!

Love

Laughter

Hugs

Childbirth

Jokes

Humour

Sight

Sharing

Hearing

Passion

Dancing

Ocean

Sunshine

Appreciation

Respect

Moonlight

Creativeness

Hope

Positive thoughts

Choice

Nature

Air

Peace & Quiet

Stars

Advice

Hope

Surprises

Singing

Wildlife

Sunrise

Sunset

Play

A smile

A whisper

Words

Encouragement

Self-development

Touch

Freedom

Fun
Fresh air
Self-belief

Love every inch of being you and remain positive, true & confident in all you choose to do!

One person can wear many different hats

Mum's hat

I put my heart and soul into raising my children to become decent members of society and it has definitely paid off. I strongly believe the first five years of a child's development is vital to all aspects of a child's future. Over the years it has been hard, lots of fun, challenging, never a dull moment, exhausting and lonely but I have no regrets and wouldn't have changed a thing. Even as they are becoming young independent adults they still need my love, guidance and motivation, that is never going to change. There are sacrifices we all make once we have children but that doesn't mean we need to resort to letting our own needs go, it is just as important to maintain your individuality. With a little reshuffling and organisation in our lives, it can be done, even if it means finding the time to meet up with friends or timeout for yourself. It is not selfish, I believe it is very important to being able to be the best parent you can.

Being a parent is a 24/7 job. Yes, it is one of the best jobs in the world, but you also need time for you.

Fun hat

I don't take life too seriously and I have fun while getting on with my journey through life. I come across so many young people in their twenties and thirties or even late teens that look so serious as if all the fun has been zapped out of them. I look younger than most of them because I'm much more young at heart than them. They all want to grow up so fast and go from 19 to 30 just like that. STOP! Incorporate a healthy balance between work, rest and play. Steer clear from negative energies and most of all don't take life too seriously. Life is for living, yes, all the other mundane everyday things that come with life need attending to, but take time out to have fun and let your hair down. Create fun memories that can be cherished for years to come. There is no age limit or restrictions on having fun or sharing the fun times with others.

Sassy hat

I 'm still a woman who wants to feel sexy & classy and just because I'm a mum, that shouldn't take my unique individuality away. I love the baggy t-shirt and tracksuit bottoms now and then for cosy home days but I have my sassy days too. I take care of myself from within and I'm a woman who isn't afraid to show off her curvy side. Even if it's wearing a lipstick or painting your nails, believe me, simple things can make us feel great about ourselves.

Don't take Life too seriously, believe me you'll enjoy the journey a lot more!

My three Rs rules

- **R***esponsible*-I am the only one responsible for my journey in my life and my wellbeing

- **R***ealistic*-I must have a realistic plan in establishing my chosen lifestyle to achieve all I desire

- **R***espond*-I have a duty to respond to my goals and ambitions in life

Feel Young

Be young

Stay young

It's all in the planning

T ry to plan ahead as much as possible, I know it might seem a little regimented but organisation can remove a lot of stress and save a lot of time in the long run. We will have more time to enjoy living if we have a bit more organisation in our lives. We all put a lot of thought, time and energy into planning our perfect holiday. Even if the holiday doesn't turn out to match the dream holiday in our minds, we've planned it, we've researched it, discussed it and worked hard to pay for it. Why? Because we know how much we deserve it and need a relaxing break.

We daydream about the whole experience and relaxation that we're going to experience. We visualise everything from the beverages and food that are going to be on offer for us to indulge in, to the entertainment and wonderful experiences we're going to share with loved ones. We see ourselves relaxing and becoming less and less stressed as the holiday mode begins to really kick in. As the departure day to return home looms ever so closer, the stress starts to creep back in. It's as if we've given the stress and the worries of everyday life time off too. I understand life has to go back to the normal rat race but with a little planning put in place, it could be a lot less stressful and much more enjoyable. Think about your workplace, whether it be an office based job or a catering establishment. There is a routine, a plan, and a schedule and job role for every member of the team, from the head chef to the kitchen porter. In the office the cleaner is allocated a certain timeslot and the Finance Administrator has to prioritise their working day to meet deadlines. Everyone has a key part to play to make certain of productive time management. This enables a successful running of the workplace and most of all reduces stress and hopefully has a happy well managed working environment.

Talking from a single parent's point of view, I have to plan ahead and have some form of structure to reduce my stress levels and not spend all my time with a duster in one hand and handcuffed to the kitchen sink with the other. I love living and I want to get as much out of being healthy and alive as possible. I aim for a clutter free mind each night as I go to bed. That doesn't mean I have nothing on my to do list, it means I have written down what I need to do and it's there for the next day. That way I can go to bed with a clear and uncluttered mind, aiding a good night's sleep.

My Needs

- Reduce stress to the minimum
- Have a well-balanced social life
- Alone time
- Spend quality time with loved ones
- Have one to ones with my children
- Love my children equally and support them 24/7
- Enhance my personal & professional growth
- Maintain regular physical activities

- Maintain a healthy mind, body & soul
- Maintain a regular healthy eating plan
- Treat myself to beauty & relaxing treatments
- Holidays
- Keep my finances in check
- Enjoy, appreciate and most of all, love myself and my life!

My Children's needs

- Unconditional Love
- Sense of responsibility
- Learn life skills
- Dealing with peer pressure
- Focus on education and career paths
- Coping with hormonal and body changes
- Discovering the alien world of working and responsibility
- Keeping up with the crazy world of social media
- Discovering their own individualities, ideas, interests and fashion

So taking everyone's needs into account I have to have some form of organisation in both my life and the home. A must have for me is a rota for household chores, which I divide up equally among the family. This removes any unnecessary arguments about whose turn it is to do the washing up or clean the bathroom, for example. Everyone has to take their turn in maintaining a clean house. I always tell my children I don't expect a tidy house 24/7 but there is no excuse for not having a clean house. A well balanced eating plan is very important for me and my children. Having a variety of healthy meals that I've pre-planned means I can satisfy everyone and keep the weekly shopping bill down. Having drawn up weekly menus means I'm not rushing around the supermarket like a headless chicken trying to plan meals in my head and avoid a head to head trolley collision.

The problems I've found with not planning meals ahead are:

- Can end up spending more money than you anticipated
- Can end up buying duplicates
- Getting stressed as you are planning meals there and then in your head
- Making unhealthy choices
- Getting distracted by special promotions
- Impulsive buying
- Taking longer in the shop than necessary
- Repeating unnecessary shopping trips

Get organised and start living more!

Who do you love more, you or your car?

T hink of your body like a car, it sounds crazy but hear me out. You buy a nice shiny car, whether it be brand new or second hand, it is yours. You've saved up and worked hard and earned it. Going back to inside out for a moment, imagine seeing a Ferrari; a nice red shiny one drive past you. Now the internal mechanical work that went into creating that beauty is what gives the car its speed, sound and smoothness. Then the" make up", the outer shell of the car is added last, but the real beauty of the car is held from within. Even the most novice of us know we can't just jump in our vehicles daily and drive without fuel and regular maintenance. You know you need to invest in your car to get the best out of it and avoid expensive mechanical problems along the way. The exterior might be all sparkly and shiny but that is not going to get you from A to B if the internal parts are not in good working order. It will soon start to fall apart and that sparkly new car will quickly become known as that unreliable old banger that is more trouble than it's worth. It is down to you to take responsibility to spend time and money to maintain your car to get the best out of your investment long term.

Car essentials

- Fuel
- Water
- Oil
- M.O.T.
- Decent tyres
- Temperature checks
- Regular service
- Body work
- Screen protection

Human essentials

- Air
- Water
- Food
- Regular activities
- Rest
- Happiness
- Love
- Sun
- Healthy eating pattern

Comparing the running of a car against maintaining the running of you, who are you giving more attention to? Who are you relying on more in your daily life? Treat your body with the TLC (tender, loving, care) it deserves and it'll reward you and be reliable as your car.

You as an individual are the best investment you can make, you are the only one who can make the right choices for you.

Don't see it as a short term investment, like a seasonal quick fix, you're in it for the long term. Everyone is a unique individual and remember what lifestyle works for Diana in human resources will not necessarily work for Susan on reception. Don't be a sheep with YOUR BODY & LIFE, it's yours and there is no return policy. You are the sole and proud owner, own it and love every inch of it!

You wouldn't inject the wrong fuel into your car, so be more aware about what you fuel your body with!

Be more appreciative and keep a Positive Mind set

When I ask people what makes them happy the answer is usually the same: "Not a lot". They are not appreciative of all they already possess, yet they want more riches in life. I am truly thankful for all I have in my life, from my children to the roof over our heads. Be appreciative of what you have in your life today and remain positive about things to come in the future. Remember people come and people go, someone that you may believe is a positive aspect in your life yesterday may not be today. From a young age I was very inquisitive like a sponge absorbing everything around me. I wanted to be firmly in the middle of everything and always be a part of what was going on. As time has gone on I have decided to decipher what is a positive influence and what is harmful for me. It's like a continuous rotating belt of monitoring my intake of my environment and also who I surround myself with. I have friends that I have contact with via social media and then those who I actually socialise with. So I can still have contact with a majority of people but I'm not surrounding myself with other people's dramas and negative energies. Remaining positive at all times helps me to cope when stressful situations occur. Perseverance with a positive mind set is a very powerful tool for us all. I never give up on my dreams, I re-evaluate, dust down, keep my head held high and carry on.

How I felt yesterday will not determine how I will feel today!

ABC to a positive life

Abundance

Bounce back

Confidence

Dynamic

Energised

Fulfilment

Grateful

Harmonious

Intuitive

Joyous

Kind

Limitless

Motivated

Nurturing

Optimistic

Prosperous

Quality

Radiant

Self-reliant

Thankful

Unique

Versatile

Worthy

Youthful

Zesty

Surround yourself

With

People & images

that make you

smile

Achieving personal goals

- Believe in yourself, when others might doubt you
- Be positive about who you are today and each and every day
- Be able to remain focused & clear about your goals in your life
- Be open to change and redirecting your journey through life
- Become the one who loves being you every single day

Don't let people's own issues and opinions bombard you with negative thoughts and blockages on **your** own personal journey.

When I set my mind, body and soul to achieve a personal goal one thing I avoid doing is seeking the green light from others. I keep my personal goals and dreams to myself. I don't require the whole world to know what I'm aiming to achieve as it is personal to me. We all have opinions and sometimes we can be easily distracted or led to believe we are aiming above and beyond. Especially when everyone wants to voice their opinions, they can lead to negativity and self doubt in our minds. When I fell pregnant with my twins everyone had an opinion, from how was I going to carry twins full term to how was I going to cope looking after four young children. Well I went full term and delivered two healthy weight babies naturally. I have brought up four well-mannered and behaved children that are an asset to society as well as myself. So once you have the right mind set and the determination, you can succeed in whatever your own personal goals are! Start replacing negative thoughts with positive thoughts, TODAY! If you keep thinking negatively you are only encouraging negative thoughts to remain.

I made the decision to become healthier, knowledgeable and remain at a healthy weight that worked for me. I know that being happy and enjoying my life my way is what makes me content. It wasn't easy and it was a rocky road but I remained focused and determined. I wasted money, time, made mistakes and made impulsive decisions along the way. I just kept picking myself up and discovering what worked and what was realistic for me. My mindset always worked in sync with my body, visualising a happier, healthier, and positive me. I always and still have a clear mental image of the outcome I continue to achieve.

Having a clear visual image in my head helped me become more confident and at peace with myself. Avoiding drama creators can be so refreshing and frees up time for you. If you start to feel bogged down with other people's issues and negativities then it is time to re-evaluate.

Achieving my personal goals

There is no shame
in loving yourself
as this must be
accomplished
before you look to
others to return
the love

Love yourself unconditionally

We all need to accept who we are and the way we look. I always tell my children, you must love yourself before you look to others for love and acceptance. I wasn't brought up where love was given out freely and I never felt the feeling of being loved. I grew up believing that loving myself would be frowned upon and not a normal thought process. As soon as I gave birth to my first child I made certain my child knew the understanding of being loved, loving others and loving themselves. I'm not ashamed or big headed when I say I love being me 100%. I don't think I'm the best thing since sliced bread, it means I accept myself for who I am, flaws and all. I don't wish to aspire to be anyone else or follow the latest trends. By embracing and totally appreciating who I am as a unique individual, keeps me positive, content and above all happy in my own skin. When I hear people say "I wish I could look and be like so and so", it really concerns me as to why anyone would desire to be someone else. Focus on living your life and embrace your unique qualities, be true to who you are. If there are certain obstacles that might be holding you back then address them and stop putting them off. Start living, enjoying and loving who you are today!

GREAT benefits always start from within!

Nourish from inside to see the effects on the outside.

L ooking after my body from within is my biggest tip I can give you. If I can maintain a fit, happy and healthy me from inside it will and does show on the outside. I can then add the make up to enhance the good work I've done from within and feel great as well as look good. Make up will always be at our disposal but our mind, body and souls need to be regularly maintained. I believe in natural beauty rather then what I call plasterboard beauty. I see so many females with full make up on going to work or going about their everyday business, but they look so miserable. Shouldn't they be glowing and feeling like a million pounds with their perfectly applied make up on? All the time and skill it takes to apply good make up and they look like they've just lost a winning lottery ticket. They have very negative characteristics, they're grumpy, snappy, lack energy, have very little or no sense of humour and their physical appearance are all signs they need a serious M.O.T. from within!

Make long term reachable, realistic & beneficial lifestyle choices, not one hit wonders that you know you are unable to sustain

A laugh a day keeps
the wrinkles away

I love to laugh

A laugh a day keeps the wrinkles and stress away. We all encounter stressful situations in our day to day hectic lives, this is part of life full stop! Will getting stressed and worrying over our problems and dilemmas make any difference? No!

Don't get me wrong I don't brush my problems under the carpet and hope they'll go away, on the other hand I don't let them bog me down either. I find laughter a great stress release as well as a timeout is also a great distraction from focusing on the negatives, guilt and frustrations of just living. I don't take myself too seriously, I believe it is a great characteristic to have and I wouldn't change it for all the tea in China. We all know at least one or more hard faced sourpuss who fears that if they crack a smile or show any sign of humour, their face will crack and their whole regimented world would collapse. Those are the people that have red alert written all over them, they are also the people that look and act double their age. GET A SENSE OF HUMOUR! I feel like I've got two heads when I'm out in public and my laughter can be overheard. People turn around with great speed as if the sound of laughter is a very unfamiliar sound. Then comes the stare, the stare that reads stop laughing, stop having enjoyment or I wish I could be free and as confident to be in your shoes right now.

You know that feeling when you've got tears rolling down your face and you feel like you can't even catch your breath, WOW! that is the best feeling and remedy in the world and it's free for all. Think about how good you feel after the laughter has calmed down, you've just had a great physical tension, stress and emotional release. Your muscles will be relaxed for up to 45 minutes after the laughter has stopped.

Laughter is a fantastic antidote for building and bonding emotionally with others. I raised all my children on good old laughter, it definitely played a positive part in building our everlasting loving relationships. I use humour as a way of dealing with resentments, jealousy, emotional & physical pain. Incorporating laughter within relationships with loved ones as well as people at work can dramatically enhance the relationships and keep them fresh, triggering positive emotions and a stress free zone.

Seeing a baby smile for the first time is a wonderful experience, babies begin smiling within their first weeks of life. That is quickly followed with the beautiful sound of laughter within their first few months. There is no reason why smiling, laughter and having a good sense of humour should halt because we've grown up.

Health benefits from laughter

- Laughter releases physical tension and muscle tightness, leaving your muscles relaxed up to 45 minutes after the laughter has ceased.
- Laughter is great in boosting the immune system, stress hormones are reduced while immune cells and infection-fighting antibodies are increased, aiding your body's resistance to disease.
- Laughter triggers endorphins to be released which are the body's natural feel-good chemicals, enhancing an

overall sense of well-being and can even temporarily relieve pain and depression.

- Laughter is a great heart protector by improving the function of the blood vessels which in turn increases the blood flow to the heart.

Mental health benefits from laughter

- Feelings of anxiousness, anger, sadness, low self-worth, depression can be dramatically reduced by laughter.
- Laughter helps you to chill out/relax and recharge your body, leading to reduced stress levels and improving your energy levels. It enables you to have a much clearer thought process and to achieve more.
- Bring laughter into your life and share contagious laughter with others.

Smiling is pleasing to the eye which leads to a great feeling of comfortableness for those around you. As soon as I meet someone I smile, I walk into a room of strangers with a great big smile on my face. This helps set the tone, without even having a verbal conversation with someone the mood is set. People are more likely to engage with each other if they are greeted with a warm welcoming smile rather than a standoffish demeanour.

So many times I hear the words "I have nothing to laugh about" or "Why are you laughing? It's not funny". Because I love my life, I appreciate the things I have and I feel positive about each new day and what joy and happiness awaits me. I am not going to stay focused on the negatives in my life which is only going to place a barrier to enjoying each day with humour and laughter. Most of the time we all have a choice in who and what environment we chose to surround ourselves with. I thrive on humorous individuals who laugh easily and don't take themselves or life too seriously.

Reasons to make you laugh

- Laughter is contagious
- Triggers the release of endorphins
- Produces an overall sense of well being
- Decreases stress hormones, depression, fear, anxiety and tension
- Enhances a happy mood
- Helps maintain a healthy heart, relaxes the muscles
- Builds positive bonds with others
- An attractive characteristic
- Reduces conflict
- Laughter is the best free medicine you can get
- Helps boost the immune system
- Helps a healthy heart
- Laughter adds spice to life, like cream to a cake

Quick tips to make you laugh

- Watch a funny movie or TV show, search the internet for stand up comedians
- Go to a comedy club, even if the acts aren't good you can still laugh at them
- Surround yourself with funny people
- Share a good joke or a funny story
- Girls/lads night in with friends
- Get a pet, as pets can do the funniest things
- Join in with the kids by having fun and turn back the hands of time
- Do something silly and out of character

- Lose your inhibitions
- Make time for fun activities and have a balance between work and play
- Try and be spontaneous at times
- Be expressive
- Lower the defence wall

Express yourself, don't suppress yourself

Drink it and lots of it

Water is definitely a must have for me every day, even at weekends when good habits tend to go out the window. The recommended amount is 1.5L/ 8 glasses a day. Try to space your intake of water out throughout the day, to avoid over flooding your system and getting that bloated feeling. There are so many varieties of water available in the shops, the choice is yours. Room temperature is easier on your insides than refrigerated water.

Quick tip-Replace two glasses of water after one cup of tea or coffee to avoid dehydration.

Benefits of drinking water-

- Transports nutrients and oxygen into cells
- Reduces hunger
- Hydrates the body which can ease back pain and headaches
- Moisturises the air in the lungs
- Helps with metabolism
- Protects our vital organs
- Helps our organs to absorb nutrients better
- Regulates body temperature
- Detoxifies aiding weight loss
- Protects and moisturises our joints

- Helps to replenish skin tissue, moisturises skin which increases skin elasticity, leaving a youthful and younger looking you
- Helps with a better digestion system
- Helps prevent constipation
- Helps keeps you healthier and staying more focused
- Relieves fatigue and reduces the likelihood of illness
- Zero calories
- Water is great at helping to fuel your muscles and regulate your body temperature while exercising. It gives you more energy during exercise when you need it most
- Dilutes cancer causing agents reducing the risk of colon cancer and bladder cancer
- Reduces cramps and sprains
- signs that you need to drink more water-
- Dark Urine – Dark Yellow or Orange in Colour: Urine is generally pale yellow to clear when you have sufficient water intake. Dark colour or strong smell indicates that you need to drink more water
- Dry Skin: Skin is our largest body organ and requires a good amount of water
- Thirst: Thirst is the most obvious sign that you're already dehydrated. It is always a good practice to drink more water when you are not thirsty, don't wait until you're thirsty
- Hunger: Most people mistake hunger for the indication to eat more, whereas in actual fact, they may be dehydrated. So before you have your meal, grab a glass of water
- Fatigue: Water is a source of energy and gives you a boost in energy

Yellow and bright but bitter to bite

W arm water with a squeeze of lemon is one of my morning glories.

Each morning I start my day with a warm glass of water and a squeeze of a half a fresh lemon. I always brush my teeth beforehand and use a straw to protect my teeth from the acid damaging my teeth enamel. I also rinse my mouth with water straight afterwards. Try making a jug of water with some lemon slices added to it, to get even more benefits.

Benefits of the almighty lemon

- Great liver detoxifier
- Helps with stomach cramps and flatulence
- Aids a good bowel movement
- Helps in weight loss due to the high levels of pectin fibre, which help with hunger cravings
- The citric acid in lemons helps to dissolve gallstones, calcium deposits and kidney stones
- Lemons help restore balance to the body's PH
- Lemons are one of the best sources of alkaline foods available
- Rich in vitamin C and flavonoids which help neutralise free radicals linked to aging and other diseases

- Helps against colds and flu
- Destroys intestinal worms
- Great aid for digestion
- Helps to keep your urinary tract healthy by increasing the rate of urination, which helps to purify it
- Blood vessels are strengthened by the vitamin P (bioflavonoids) which can help with high blood pressure
- Lemons contain 22 anti-cancer compounds
- Helps to give your immune system a boost
- Helps in bad breath

Brush those bumps away every day

O ur skin is our biggest organ and is the first to show signs of aging.

I dry body brush twice daily and always before showering, especially in the morning. I start at the base of my foot sweeping upwards always towards the heart, with a light hand not to mark the skin.

Benefits of dry body brushing

- Increases blood circulation & lymphatic drainage by the release of toxins
- Helps reduce the appearance of cellulite
- Rejuvenates the nervous system by stimulating the nerve endings in the skin
- Helps in removing dead skin and encourages new cells to renew
- It helps with muscle tone and gives you a more even distribution of fat deposits
- Can help with removal of ingrowing hairs
- Dry skin brushing helps your skin to absorb nutrients by eliminating clogged pores
- Helps to leave skin looking fresh and perky

- Power nap
- Shuteye
- Snooze
- Cat nap
- Siesta
- Rest
- Recovery time
- Timeout
- Quiet time

- My alone time

Sleeping beauty

I don't play when it comes to my sleep (I love to sleep and rejuvenate) and I truly believe this has played a major part in keeping me looking young and fresh. I listen to my body and I have one simple rule, when my eyes are heavy and my body is tired, I don't fight it. I avoid reaching for a quick caffeine hit just to watch the end of a film or because the clock hasn't struck midnight. I'm off to bed in a flash and I try to avoid going into sofa sleep mode, by going to bed at any hour.

I want to feel rejuvenated the next day not dragging myself out of bed and looking worse for wear. Around eight hours a night is what my body deserves as well as time out during the day when possible.

Quick Tip

Make your appointments first thing in the morning when possible, as you are more likely to receive a much more pleasant and better quality of service.

Benefits of getting adequate sleep zzzzz

- Reduce the aging process
- Gain a better quality of life
- Reduce the risk of diabetes
- Aid with weight loss
- Improve a better working memory
- Maintain a healthy heart
- Reduce stress levels
- Live longer

- Repair the body's organs
- Keep depression and mood swings at bay
- Awake feeling more alert and creative. Always aim for some peaceful timeout alone time during the day

I do some deep breathing to send soothing messages to my brain that it's time to switch off. By breathing in for the count of five and out for the count of five helps me to focus on my breath. By slowing down my thought process this allows me to switch off. Some say that having a nap/timeout during the day can add years to your life expectancy. There is **_no_** excuse not to be able to find five minutes during the day. So you have meetings booked back to back, do it on the bus/train or plane, the cleaning cupboard, the car, just find the time and you'll feel like a new you. It's amazing how we can find time to make that quick call that probably could have been made later or to go for that sneaky cigarette, which is really a signal that you need to breathe in and exhale. We can fit in a visit to the coffee machine but we don't have the time or willpower to give ourselves five minutes to just breathe.

I certainly feel the benefits all over.

My little bit of magic in a capsule

Evening Primrose oil 1000g

I used to suffer from severe eczema to the point that my whole face was swollen, cracked and itchy, my skin would constantly be weeping and I was in so much discomfort it was unbearable. I went to the doctor crying out for some miracle relief but I was handed prescriptions for creams that contained steroids. This was a true wake up call for me and I had to really look at the causes and start to educate myself, to help myself.

I went to my local Chinese herbalist after no success with conventional medicines. I was given a two week course of herbal teas that within days restored my skin to that of a new born baby and I was finally eczema free. To be able to maintain my new found outer beauty I had to make certain changes to my diet from within. I started with cutting out the good old English cup of tea, cakes, biscuits, citrus fruits i.e. green apples & kiwi, chocolate and even cow's milk. I had indulged in these baddies throughout my childhood and into my teens. My body was rejecting them and I had to start looking into alternatives that worked for me.

I had suffered at least three extreme cases of constipation as a child that at one point I turned a pale shade of white and needed urgent medical assistance. So this was a clear indication that my body was very sensitive to what I put in it and I needed to start paying more attention to my eating habits.

A male friend of mine suggested I start taking Evening Primrose oil and also applying it topically to my face and hands before bed. I immediately started taking two 1,000mg capsules daily without fail and this I would say has really been my beneficial secret to looking so young. At the time I started taking Evening Primrose oil I honestly didn't realise the great benefits this would have on my skin twenty years on.

Benefits of Evening Primrose oil

- Great source of omega 6 fatty acid called gamma linoleic acid GLA
- Helps with premenstrual syndrome and menopausal symptoms
- Breast cancer-There has been some research that has suggested the GLA may help destroy tumours without inducing damage to normal cells or causing harmful side effects
- Helps against topical eczema. Evening primrose oil may help relieve the itching, crusting, redness, and swelling due to the fatty acids can play a role in these beneficial effects
- Helps against the aging process and maintaining a youthful appearance
- May help those suffering from severe headaches
- Great for keeping acne at bay
- Helps with hyperactivity in children (I give my 15 year old son one capsule a day)
- Aids weight control

Vitamin C and E both work wonders for me

Vitamin C to the rescue, I was first introduced to the amazing benefits of taking vitamin C consistently in my early/mid twenties. I used to suffer from really dry cracks at the side of my mouth as well as really dry lips. I was told I was lacking vitamin C and had a nutritional deficiency. I take the water-soluble version with water daily, especially if I begin to feel the dryness returning around my mouth.

Quick tip -Add some honey and lemon if you're beginning to feel the sniffles coming on

Great benefits of taking vitamin C

- Helps to protect cells from free radicals and keep them nice and healthy in the prevention of aging, diabetes some types of cancer and tissue damage
- Plays an important part in collagen production leading to benefits to aid wound healing
- May help in the protection from free radicals caused by exposure to UV (ultraviolet) rays
- Supports the immune system which is the first defence against cancer cells forming. Aids the

immune system to stay nourished and defends against cancer

- Helps the increase of iron we can absorb from greens, such as broccoli, kale and sprouts
- Antioxidants that can help protect us from damage caused by exposure such as pollution, pesticides, tobacco smoke and harmful sun rays
- Helps reduce the risk of cataracts, counteracting the free radicals from sunlight direct to the eyes
- 1,000 mg per day of vitamin C
- Take it regularly to keep colds and flu away
- Can help prevent heart disease from halting free radicals from damaging the artery walls

Vitamin E

In terms of skin health and skin care, the vitamin E benefits are numerous. There are so many skin care products that contain vitamin E that help play an essential part in maintaining healthy skin. The antioxidant activity in vitamin E is vital in protecting skin cells from ultra violet light, pollution, drugs, and other elements that produce cell damaging free radicals. It is believed that vitamin E is most effective in its natural alcohol form rather than its acetate form where it is a less effective antioxidant. Watch for this in the labelling of skin care products.

Acupuncture

A cupuncture has been around and played a major part in ancient Chinese medicine for thousands of years. There are a number of health benefits that having regular acupuncture can bring. I find that regular acupuncture sessions help ease my lower back pain and improve my digestive system. Acupuncture is now being widely used by western doctors, for its health benefits. Prices vary, so shop around and ask your GP if they offer it. Some practitioners offer a multi bed service, where there are a number of patients being treated at the same time. Although you don't have the privacy of your own room, there is a screen that separates the patients. This method helps reduce the price of treatment.

Ginkgo Biloba

G inkgo Biloba is used across the world and holds so many amazing health benefits. I started using it to improve brain and memory function. After four children I needed a little brain and memory booster. I take one Ginkgo Biloba & ginseng extract oral liquid vial each morning followed by warm water. I can feel the difference instantly and I'm immediately alert and raring to embrace my day ahead. Many health shops sell the tablet form and I tend to give my children the tablet form as there is no bitter aftertaste that you get with the vials. If they are taking an exam or need that extra brain boost then I'll give them the vial. I used to suffer from really painful cramps and unbearable pain in my lower legs and my elbows, but since taking Ginkgo Biloba, the pain has gone. The Chinese have been using Ginkgo Biloba for an array of health benefits for thousands of years.

Benefits of taking Ginkgo Biloba

- Great benefits for Alzheimer's disease and dementia
- Helps with depression
- Menopause
- A real benefit in aiding short term memory loss and benefiting memory
- Allows for mental clarity
- Improves blood flow to the brain
- Reduces hardening of the arteries which in turn helps relax the blood vessels
- Can help improve infertility and impotence in men

- Helps protect the body from free radicals which reduces the signs of aging, while it also helps protect the body's major organs
- Traditionally used to help with those suffering from asthma, bronchitis and wheezing cough

Stop feeling guilty about self indulgence and start exploring

Massage the stress and aches away

We all love a good massage once in a while but I truly believe in having regular massages as part of my lifestyle, not just as a mother's day or birthday treat. There are so many recognised health benefits that having regular massages can bring. Massage is widely offered in hospices, intensive care units, mental health environments as well as post surgery and cancer patients. Many illnesses are induced by stress and we all know that stress can take a great toll on our bodies both internally and externally. What better way to reduce the level of stress from our bodies than indulging in a therapeutic, rejuvenating, pampering and de-stressing massage regularly. There is really no excuse these days, as there are so many discounted websites offering highly reduced body treatments.

The Benefits Of Massage

- Helps reduce back problems
- Helps you become more flexible and improve range of motion
- Stimulates lymph flow (which is the body's natural defence system)
- Could help reduce medication dependency
- Eases tightness and stretches weak and overused muscles

- Greatly improves the body's biggest organ; THE SKIN!
- Improves joint flexibility
- Reduces effects of depression, anxiety and mood related symptoms
- Promotes tissue regeneration, may help with reducing cellulite
- Improves the flow of oxygen and nutrients into tissue and vital organs
- Improves circulation
- Relieves cramps and spasms
- Helps with relief from migraines
- Endorphins are released producing feelings of euphoria and a general state of wellbeing
- Decreases anxiety
- Improves sleep patterns
- Improves energy levels

My personal favourite is Acupressure:

- A Chinese therapeutic massage which aids health and balance throughout the body
- Yin (negative energy) and Yang (positive energy) channels are regulated
- Relieves tension from muscles by stimulating the acupressure points
- Vigorous rubbing over the skin increases the blood flow
- A standing heat lamp is used to warm and relax the muscles

Straws galore

I always carry a straw in my bag, to protect my teeth from staining and tooth enamel erosion and direct contact with the front of the teeth. People often look at me funny when I ask for a herbal tea and a straw. When I'm at friends' homes I have to explain that it's not because their cups are unclean, I just like to protect my teeth as much as possible. Especially with all the dark coloured teas I drink, staining can be a big problem. Myself and my children all use straws and not just when we're out and about but in the house too. I want to protect our teeth as much as possible, especially from daily exposure to citric acid, which over time can lead to weak tooth enamel. I and my children have no fillings and always get the thumbs up from the dentist, (touch wood) may it long continue.

Quick tip-Drink some milk or eat some cheese after meals to help protect your teeth from acid erosion. Try to rinse your mouth with water after meals.

Benefits of drinking with a straw

- Protects teeth from staining
- Decreases exposure
- Hygiene from germs when out & about
- Convenience using a straw while on the go
- Safety; less likely to choke

Hold your head up
a little higher

&

Walk a little taller

Walk the walk

Walking is such a major milestone in a baby's development and a great moment when we see a child take their first steps. So why is it that we forget how powerful simple walking can benefit us all. I remember walking while on holiday abroad and literally being stared at as if I was out of space. I was then informed that it was very unusual for people to be seen walking, hence the increase of obesity. We all need to be active in some shape or form and walking is the perfect tool to use to keep in shape. As soon as we learn to drive walking seems to go out the window, even searching for the nearest parking spot to the shops seems to be a must have for us. Walking shouldn't been seen as a chore, more like a part of our everyday lifestyle. In the quiet of the morning there is nothing I enjoy doing more than taking a quick fast paced walk, to gear me up for the day ahead.

Walking is a major part of my lifestyle and even when I'm having a rest day off doing my activity, I'll make sure I have a brisk walk.

Benefits of power walking

- It's FREE! No membership required!
- Great form of activity for all ages & fitness abilities
- Great way to start becoming more active as a family or with friends
- Aids weight loss
- Helps clear the mind & reduce stress
- Helps you stay focused

- Tones up the bum, legs and arms while you power walk
- Helps with maintaining good posture
- Walking regularly helps reduce chronic illnesses, heart disease, type 2 diabetes, asthma, strokes and some forms of cancers
- An aerobic form of activity so your heart rate is raised and you're slightly breathless

Tips to stay motivated and keen to walk

- Alone time
- Save on petrol
- A chance to have a catch up with friends & loved ones on hands free calls away from listening ears
- A chance to learn while you walk
- Get off the bus / train a stop earlier
- Park the car furthest away from the shops
- Walk to work or at least park the car further away from work
- Walk to the local shops instead of jumping in the car
- Take the stairs instead of the lift
- Go for a romantic walk with a loved one
- Go for an after dinner walk to help you sleep well
- Go for an early morning walk to blow away the cobwebs
- Sightseeing while you're being active
- Treat yourself to a pair of new trainers

Facial workout

We all know the benefits of working out has on our bodies, how about a little thought for our face?

Having a good old stretch from head to toe feels great and we are left feeling rejuvenated. I stretch my face out a few times a week and it feels wonderful and relaxed. The great thing about doing these facial exercises is they can be done anytime and anywhere. I generally fit them in while I'm washing up, stuck in traffic, while the adverts are on, lying down in bed or walking.

Tips for a good facial workout

- Open your mouth as wide as possible as well as your eyes at the same time
- Screw your whole face up as tight as you can hold for a few seconds then release
- Sit up straight and tilt your head back and drop your lower jaw up and down
- Smile as wide as you can & close your eyes as you smile
- Starting at your jaw line closest to your ears, use two or three finger tips and slowly massage inwards and upwards in small circular movements
- Press your lips together (as if you're puckering up for a kiss) then turn your mouth to either side
- Close your eyes one at a time by lifting up your cheek bones (like you're giving an over exaggerated wink)

Face the facts

I haven't always cared and had the knowledge I now have for caring for my face on a daily basis. So here is my daily skin care regime that I now maintain.

We all do it daily and sometimes we don't even realise we're doing it; touching our face. No more touchy touchy, imagine how many different forms of bacteria we are transferring from our hands to our face.

A typical day at work in an office:

- Answering the phone
- Using the keyboard
- Using the water filter
- Touching door handles
- Shaking hands with colleagues
- Touching the lift button
- Handling paperwork
- Handling cash
- Operating the general office equipment
- Holding onto the stairs or escalator rails
- Touching/playing with your hair

Then you go and touch your face which can lead to clogging up your pores and causing spots and pimples. If you are a face toucher, try to wash your hands more often and just become more aware of your habits. Habit changing can be done, so find ways that work for you!

Changing your bad habits can be achieved!

- A well thought out realistic plan, written down clearly
- Commitment
- Understanding and avoiding triggers
- Achievable goals
- Continuation for 30 days
- Helps the bad habits change their ways!

Know your skin type

I know my skin can be dry, sensitive and prone to eczema so I have to be extremely careful about what products I use on my skin. I have found products that work for me are not the ones that come with a high price tag.

What I use on my skin-

- Hand cream-Dr Organics Manuka Nail and Hand cream.
- Face cream-Dr Organic Manuka Honey Rescue Cream on my face.
- Body and hair cream-100% pure coconut oil (I buy mine from my local Asian cash and carry, so much cheaper than other retailers).

Different Skin types-

- Dry
- Sensitive
- Combination
- Normal
- Oily

My step by step daily face washing routine-

- Wash hands before you start to remove dirt to avoid transferring dirt.
- Remove the majority of makeup (if wearing makeup) with a damp cotton wool pad.
- Use a cleanser to remove dirt & oil, it helps to unclog pores to enable them to open up and breathe.
- Use a face scrub to remove dead skin cells to allow for new cells to grow, leaving skin soft and clean.

Use a sensitive cleanser and cotton pad, in a circular motion in an upwards movement, gently work upwards avoiding the sensitive eye area.

- Splash warm water on your face, using two fingers to gently rub the scrub in the same motion as the cleanser.
- Leave on the face for a minute or so.
- Rinse off with warm water.
- Pat dry with either a small facial/hand towel (that you only use for your face) or a soft disposable paper tissue.

Toner is a very important part of the process as it works to restore the skin's natural pH balance. It closes up the pores after cleansing, which is very important! It prepares the skin to be hydrated by moisturising, the next step.

- Place an adequate amount of toner on a cotton pad.
- Pat the cotton pad all over the face gently, avoiding the lips and sensitive area around the eyes.
- Do not wash off; let it settle before moving on to moisturising.

- Moisturising restores the skin's natural moisture lost in the cleansing process.
- Make sure your hands are clean.
- Using the best moisturiser for your skin type, dab an adequate amount (don't overdo it) on your fingers and slowly work your way upwards in circular movements. Remember not to drag the skin downwards, always upwards to keep the skin lifted. Leave the moisturiser to settle on the skin.
- Apply a good quality sun cream.

I use a good sun cream 24/7 and 52 weeks of the year, people usually look at me in shock when I tell them this. I don't spend half the year in the Caribbean or anything, I wish I could. The winter sun is just as powerful as the summer sun and we still need to protect our skin (especially face and hands). During the winter months the sun's rays are closer to the earth and stronger. Think about how powerful the sunlight is beaming in through the car windscreen. We protect our lips with a good lip balm during winter so don't neglect your face too. Remember ALL skin tones need protection from the sun.

- Always use a sun cream that protects from UVA (Ultraviolet A) & UVB (Ultraviolet B).
- A good sun cream protects the skin from pigmentation (dark marks on the skin), brown spots, sunburn which can lead to skin cancer in the future, blisters and peeling.

So try to maintain a good daily routine for your face morning & night.

Quick tips-

- I use a foot scrub once a week to exfoliate, a good exfoliator will do.
- I use evening primrose oil 500g before bed, a few nights during the week topically instead of my moisturiser. During the night my skin is able to soak up the goodness.
- My alone time, face pack, cucumber on the eyes, bath cushion, soothing relaxation music, scented candles, an aromatherapy bath; pure bliss.
- Treat yourself to a nice deep facial now and then, your face deserves it and so do you.

Sunny days are here to stay

C elebrities are hardly seen without their designer shades in the media these days. Wearing sunglasses can be more beneficial than just a fashion statement. A good quality pair of sunglasses protect the naked eye from harmful UV (Ultraviolet light) rays. I was born with congenital cataracts and my worst day was a bright sunny day. I just couldn't face the sunlight and I often was unable to enjoy the delights of summer. Although I've had both my lenses removed and replaced with permanent implants, I make sure I always have my sunglasses in my bag all year round. I'm not talking about any old cheap pair, I mean a good quality pair that will give my eyes the protection they need and deserve. We only have one pair of eyes and we shouldn't take them for guaranteed, start thinking about tomorrow today.

Benefits from wearing a good pair of sunglasses

- Protection from the sun's UV rays
- A great fashion accessory
- Protects the sensitive skin around the eyes, avoids crow's feet
- Protects from cancer within the eyelid Helps protect against cataracts which can lead to blindness
- A great protector against other eye conditions

- Protects the eyes from pollutions and flies

Nuts for all

I'm not a great nut lover myself but I do add three types of nuts to my daily balanced eating plan.

Benefits of Almond nuts

- Lowers the risk of heart attacks and heart disease
- Can help lower cholesterol
- Helps maintain strong bones and teeth
- Good for maintaining a good weight as they provide healthy fats
- Great in maintaining a healthy brain function
- May help reduce the risk of Alzheimer's
- Good for nourishing the nervous system

Benefits of Brazilian nuts-3 a day

- Brazil nuts are full of selenium, which can help protect the body from cancers
- Helps against heart attacks
- Can provide the body with essential vitamins and minerals

Benefits of Pumpkin seeds

- Full of vitamins, fibre, minerals and other antioxidants
- Great for a good night's sleep
- High in magnesium which is good for keeping a healthy heart
- Perfect snack replacement as they are an easily digestible protein

- Helps to stabilise blood sugar which can lead to gaining a healthy weight.
- Rich in Omega 3s
- A good source of zinc

Teas for me

I only drink herbal teas, I didn't always but over the years I've found they work for me. I use to drink "normal tea" all the time, I was a real put the kettle on, fancy a cup of tea kind of person. Now my cupboard is packed with a variety of teas ranging from fruit teas to traditional Chinese teas. Don't get me wrong I don't disagree with drinking your everyday cup of tea or coffee, it's just my personal choice. I don't drink coffee either as I got slightly hooked on it after the birth or my twins. I was having heart palpitations so listening to my body I got hypnotised and haven't touched a drop since. Here is a list of teas that I drink but I've chosen green tea to list the benefits of as I believe green tea has been the most beneficial to me.

Benefits of drinking Jasmine tea

- Drinking Jasmine tea when feeling stressed can lead to a tranquil sense of wellbeing
- Reduces the aging process
- Delicate taste
- Releases tension
- Jasmine tea has a beautiful sweet scent of the Jasmine flower

Benefits of drinking Camomile tea

- Perfect bedtime relaxing tea
- Can be used topically for a variety of skin & scalp benefits

- A great tea to drink during your menstrual cycle
- Aids good digestion & relieves stomach pains
- Has a sweet and delicate aroma & taste
- Supports the immune system

Benefits of drinking Oolong tea

- Very powerful antioxidant
- Helps reduce itching & irritation caused by eczema
- Improves the appearance of skin
- Metabolism booster
- Aids in fat burning
- Promotes a healthy heart
- Helps in strengthening bones
- Reduces the risk of cavities, tooth decay

Benefits of drinking peppermint tea

- Nice soothing menthol taste
- Helps promote a relaxed stomach and gives a calming feeling when suffering from nausea or menstrual pain
- Helps with flatulence
- Improves digestion
- Eases headaches & migraines
- Reduces stress & anxiety
- Helps with reducing bacteria & viruses
- Helps clear up nasal and congestion by inhaling

Quick tip-Next time you feel a cold coming or you just want to a facial steam add two peppermint tea bags to a steaming bowl of hot water. Use a good size towel over your head, breathe, relax and enjoy.

Benefits of drinking green tea

- A great antioxidant
- Lowers blood pressure
- Fights against cancer cells
- Helps in reducing high cholesterol
- Good for maintaining a healthy weight, by boosting the metabolism
- Can help to regulate glucose levels, great for diabetes
- Plays a role in preventing blood clots which could lead to heart disease and heart attacks
- Protects brain cells from damage, which could delay the signs of Alzheimer's and Parkinson's disease
- Could help protect teeth decay
- Can help against viral and bacterial infections
- Depression sufferers could benefit from drinking green tea
- Very beneficial for the skin and keeping those wrinkles at bay and delaying the aging process, due to the antioxidants

Quick Tip-Try not to drink too much green tea each day as it can flush out important nutrients from your body.

Benefits of drinking white tea

- Has a lower amount of caffeine
- White tea is the least processed of all teas
- High amount of disease fighting components
- Has a very high amount of catechin which is a great antioxidant leading to reduction in blood pressure
- May help in reducing the risk of many forms of cancers

- Drinking white tea regularly could lower the risk of reoccurring breast cancer
- White tea contains a high content of fluoride, which helps prevent cavities and strengthen teeth and bones
- Helps to burn body fat

In a nut shell

My daily must

haves

- Regular intake of vitamin D (especially during the less sunnier days)
- Two 1000 mg of evening primrose oil capsules
- One 1000 mg of cod liver oil
- One 1000mg Starflower oil
- One good multi vitamin (I take it at night, so my body can absorb the nutrients while I sleep)
- One 60mg Ginkgo Biloba tablet
- One to two apples a day (eat an apple before bed and it will aid a regular bowel movement)
- Something green; spinach, broccoli, kale or cabbage (mix it up in a smoothie to maintain a daily intake)
- Two cups of green tea
- 1.5 litres of filtered or bottled water
- Warm water with lemon
- Soluble Vitamin C

Put the fun back into keeping active

&

Young!

Active Activities

I don't like to use the word exercise or workout as it has the association with hard work, getting breathless and boredom. So I have renamed it "Active Activities" that I enjoy and will be able to realistically maintain, as well as look forward to. I tend to get bored rather easily so I need a good balance of AA to keep me motivated.

What I do and how I do it.

I have and love to mix up my active activities to remain active and focused and more importantly enjoy being active.

- Power walking
- Swimming
- Roller skating
- Ice skating
- Pilates
- Kick boxing
- Dance classes
- Yoga
- Rock climbing
- Trampolining
- Badminton
- Bike riding
- Home fitness DVD

Seconds on the lips

A lifetime on the

hips

No more dieting!

I prefer the term "Enjoying a balanced eating plan" rather than saying I'm going on a diet. Again it is my own way of breaking the negative connections with certain words that triggers fear in me. The word diet straight away sends signals to my brain that I will be -

- Starving myself half the time
- Unable to enjoy a delicious variety of foods
- Cutting out going out to social gatherings at the fear of temptations
- Becoming moody
- Constantly be thinking of food
- Hunting the supermarkets for certain unknown ingredients
- Cooking separate meals for myself and my children
- Dreading meals times

Now when I say to myself I will be "Enjoying a balanced eating plan from now on", key positive triggers leap out at me.

- This is a plan, having structure helps me to remain positive and focused
- I will be looking forward and ENJOYING meal times
- There will be a balance in my eating habits
- I can indulge in a treat now and then
- I am able to remain at a permanent healthy weight
- Having a social life is not off my to do list

Berry nutritious 4 me

- Strawberries

- Raspberries

- Cranberries

- Blackberries

- Blueberries

Quick tip-Any fruit with the word berry at the end is great for you.

When you eat right, you get to eat more

&

More!

Melons galore

I drink & eat a variety of melons including water melon, honeydew, cantaloupe, gala and Piel de Sapo daily as they are packed with vitamins and minerals. They are mainly made up of water content and have very few calories. I enjoy eating them and have them every day all year round.

Benefits of melons

- Great for keeping the skin firm and youthful due to its collagen contents
- Helps with maintaining a healthy weight
- They have that juicy sweetness but without the added calories
- May play a part in help with fighting off cancer
- Helps with reducing the risk of heart problems and strokes
- Great for your digestive system and keeping your bowel movement regular
- Eaten daily helps keep skin soft and can help with dry skin and eczema
- Good source of energy
- Melons can give you that full feeling for longer due to the water content

One rule works for all!

- Breakfast
- Healthy snack
- Lunch
- Healthy snack
- Dinner

Try something new
and you may have a
different view

Blindfold eating

We've all heard the saying "your eyes are bigger than your belly" and how true is that? I believe very true, as we will devour everything on a plate in front of us that we see without giving our bellies a second thought. We'll squash it all in and then say "I'm full up" or "I'm stuffed". The chances are you were stuffed, satisfied or full up a few or more mouthfuls before you scraped the plate clean. If we were to put down the knife and fork when we get that full feeling, the chances of overeating become much smaller, as will our stomachs.

Try blindfolding yourself at meal times and get reconnected with that sense of stopping when your stomach feels full. You might find that you take more time to chew and savour each mouthful as well as paying attention to your stomach.

When we're babies and toddlers we push away the aeroplane spoon heading towards our mouths when we are full. Then as we begin to grow we are told to eat everything on our plate and even promised with rewards if we do. This is the beginning of taking away our natural instinct of stopping when we're full and coming back for more when we're hungry again. We have now changed our eating habits to eating every single thing we _see_ on our plate in front of us.

My top tips to stop overeating at meal times:

• Get into a routine with meals so your body doesn't go out of sync even at weekends

- Blindfold yourself at meal times to feel when you're full up & break the habit of overeating
- Have time slots for breakfast, lunch and dinner to avoid overeating during the day
- Never starve yourself or hold out for a big meal as this could lead to your body storing food in fear of a famine coming, and you overeating
- Try to avoid eating on the move or rushing your meals
- Take your time by chewing each mouthful to savour the flavours and help with the digestion process
- Eat at a table when possible
- Enjoy your meals
- Reduce your stress levels
- Always remember another meal is just around the corner
- Stop when you're full, put that mind back into that stomach
- Small and frequently is better for you than big, bloated and stuffed

I eat a lot of fruit and vegetables 365 days a year and this has been really beneficial to keeping my skin looking so good. To keep my energy levels up, I need to have three balanced meals every day. I need to have green vegetables daily, that doesn't mean I have to have salad or broccoli with every meal. If I'm going out for dinner and I know there will be a variety of temptations then I'll ensure I have a light lunch with vegetables. I still want to enjoy a variety of treats and I'm not going to kid myself by starving myself or stop indulging in seasonal treats. If my day ahead is looking like my food choices will be limited then I'll make sure I include a handful of ready to eat spinach in my morning smoothie. Alternatively I'll prepare and take my own meals or snacks and keep myself in control of what goes in my mouth.

Start taking more
control of what
you put inside your
mouth

In a nut shell

- Start each day as a new positive day, with a positive outlook
- Never waste time mulling over the past that can't be undone
- Smiling and laughing goes a long way
- Keep to a healthy eating plan without depriving yourself of treats now and then
- Stay away from negative energy draining people
- Remove yourself from drama creators
- Don't hold back from paying someone a compliment
- Adapt to your present day surroundings
- Don't be afraid to recycle those around you once in a while
- Always remain in the driver's seat, never let others take control of the wheel
- Think positively and the world is your oyster
- Don't be afraid or ashamed to cry and reach out for help
- Remain as stress free as possible
- Life is a journey with a variety of obstacles along the way
- Don't be afraid of change, embrace it
- Share your experience and encourage others around you
- Remind yourself every day that you are blessed in a variety of ways
- Strive to be the best but don't beat yourself up if objectives are not achieved instantly

• # LOVE YOURSELF!

Don't stress about life
Just try your best to
Enjoy it!